Little Helpers
Toddler Cookbook

Little Helpers
Toddler Cookbook

HEALTHY, KID-FRIENDLY RECIPES TO COOK TOGETHER

Heather Wish Staller

Little Helpers
Toddler Cookbook

HEALTHY, KID-FRIENDLY
RECIPES TO COOK TOGETHER

Heather Wish Staller

PHOTOGRAPHY BY EVI ABELER

ROCKRIDGE PRESS

Interior and Cover Designer: Jami Spittler
Photo Art Director: Sue Bischofberger
Editor: Ada Fung
Production Editor: Erum Khan
Cover photography © 2019 Darren Muir. Food styling by Yolanda Muir.
Interior photography © 2019 Evi Abeler. Food styling by Albane Sharrard.
Cover: Frozen Watermelon "Pizza" Pops, p. 112

ISBN: Print 978-1-64152-476-6 | eBook 978-1-64152-477-3

To my boys,
Jack, Henry,
and Kyle

contents

Broccoli-Cheddar Cornbread Muffins, page 97

introduction

When I was four, my mom pushed a stool up to the stove and taught me how to safely make my own scrambled eggs. I remember feeling so proud that I made my own breakfast. As I got older, I would help make pancakes with my special secret ingredient (orange juice) and concocted different salad dressings for our nightly family dinner. The kitchen was a place for me to flex my creativity, feel ownership, and develop confidence. My positive experiences in the kitchen led me to pursue a career in the culinary arts, and later drew me to become a cooking instructor dedicated to passing on my love of food and cooking to children.

When I became a parent, I knew cooking with my kids would be an important part of our lives. However, my two energetic boys are two years apart, and I soon realized that it can be pretty overwhelming to make dinner on a busy night while also trying to include my boys in the cooking process. Over the years, I've come up with some clever strategies to get my kids helping in the kitchen without causing me too much stress.

I have also created lots of tried-and-true, kid-approved recipes that I've tested out in my preschool cooking classes and at home. In fact, this year I got the chance to make my Super Green Spaghetti (page 75) with my three-year-old, Henry, and his preschool class. My boys are pretty good eaters, but do I have the only child in this country who refuses to eat pasta? He won't even eat mac and cheese! So I was pretty interested to see what would happen when we made this spaghetti recipe together with his classmates. The class went well, and the kids loved chopping the veggies, zesting and juicing the lemon, and helping me stir the sauce together in my electric skillet. Of course, not all the kids liked the pasta, but at least they all tried it—including my pasta hater! I've learned that kids are much more likely to try new foods or previously rejected foods if they're allowed to take part in the cooking process. If they don't buy in right away, then maybe you'll have better success a couple of months down the road, if you keep trying and cooking together.

There are so many good reasons to cook with our kids, starting with the fact that it's great quality time. This experience also gives kids appreciation for real, wholesome ingredients and the tools to create meals out of them, which sets a foundation for a healthier future. If they're in the kitchen watching the action, they will naturally want to start playing with ingredients and doing simple tasks. The toddler age group, particularly between the ages of two and four, is a wonderful time for children to start really getting involved with preparing meals. Toddlers love to help their parents! They learn about the world from watching us and want to join in to be a part of the process. We can encourage their natural curiosity by making the kitchen safe, interactive, and fun.

Ah, yes, the mess. There's no avoiding it, so try welcoming it to the best of your ability. Cooking with toddlers is going to be messy, and you might lose your patience from time to time. But like anything else, cooking with little ones takes practice and a patient mind-set, as well as a sense of humor. In this book, I will give you the tools and support to start slow and gain confidence with each recipe you try together. At this point, it's really about the experience. Being together, getting hands "dirty" and feeling the ingredients, stirring and mashing, decorating, garnishing, and, of course, tasting. Make the kitchen a happy place, and positive experiences and delicious food will be the result!

Heather :)

Happy Cooking!

HOW TO USE THIS BOOK

The recipes are divided into five chapters: Breakfast, Lunch, Dinner, Snacks & Sides, and Desserts. Within each chapter, you'll see three levels of recipe difficulty—level 1, level 2, and level 3—but keep in mind that every recipe in this book was designed specifically to cook with toddlers. Younger toddlers or children with less cooking experience may need more assistance doing certain steps, but there are always ways to keep any child involved in the recipe. Here is a description of each recipe level to better inform your recipe choices:

Level 1: Great for beginners. Recipes are quick to prepare, so they are best for kids with shorter attention spans or those more hesitant to get cooking. Simple preparation or use of a child-safe knife may be involved for one or two ingredients. No raw eggs or stove-top cooking involved.

Level 2: Try these recipes after cooking together a few times. Recipes may involve more chopping or steps that require toddler independence. A few level 2 recipes require some stove-top cooking, but use your discretion as to how much your toddler participates in those steps.

Level 3: Best for older toddlers or more confident, interested "chefs." Recipes involve chopping or preparing several items and/or time at the stove. Of course, child-safe knives and supervised caution at the stove are still essential. A level 3 recipe will have a longer "active time," but you can always do some of the prep work on your own and involve your toddler in just a few of the steps to accommodate shorter attention spans.

Each step is color-coded, distinguishing steps that kids can likely do from those that adults should take the lead on. However, you know your child best

and should judge for yourself what parts of the recipe he is best suited to do. Recipe instructions are color-coded as follows:

1 Steps for Kids   **2 Steps for Adults**

Every recipe in this book includes tips that offer guidance, whether it be on teaching your child cooking skills, making it more fun, or avoiding common pitfalls.

Technique Tips will explain specific cooking skills such as chopping peppers, cracking eggs, or mixing ingredients without everything flying out of the bowl.

Heads Up Tips will let you know about any tricky steps or common problems that may arise while cooking, such as sticky fingers or trying to cut a tough vegetable.

Make It Fun! Tips will give you ideas for how to make your time cooking the recipe even more fun and engaging for your child, such as mashing bananas in a bag or integrating counting activities into the process.

Every recipe has a space for you and your child to note when you first made the recipe together, rate the recipe, and record what you enjoyed. There's also a section for you to jot down any additional recipe notes you might have. How fun will it be to look back and see how your child's tastes, likes, and dislikes have evolved over time? It makes this book a culinary keepsake, so you can forever relish the first memories you made with your little one in the kitchen.

All recipes are labeled dairy-free, egg-free, gluten-free, nut-free, vegetarian, and/or vegan when appropriate, so you can work around any allergies or dietary restrictions. Many recipes include substitutions for common allergens.

Just like any skill, cooking with children takes practice. Focus on having fun and making yummy foods together. You and your little chef(s) will be grinning from ear to ear when you share the recipes you've created together. Happy cooking!

Let's Cook!

I believe it's never too early to get kids in the kitchen. Sure, toddlers come with their particular set of challenges, but their natural curiosity and desire for independence make it a perfect stage of development for them to begin exploring in the kitchen—with supervision and guidance. And, of course, they want to spend time doing fun things with you! Are you looking for more ways to entertain your toddler, work on language skills and motor skills, build confidence, and foster enthusiasm for healthy eating? Cooking together can achieve all that and more.

I'm so excited that you are interested in getting in the kitchen and cooking with kids! I've been teaching kids to cook in the classroom and cooking with my own kids for years, and I can't wait to help make your time in the kitchen more fun. Toddlers can be unpredictable and full of energy, but we can find fun ways for any child to help participate in cooking. With the recipes in this book, your toddler will help you prepare delicious whole foods, including lots of fruits and vegetables, and learn about cooking techniques like a true chef!

Here are some great reasons to get toddlers cooking:

They're exposed to fruits, vegetables, and other healthy ingredients. Healthy eating starts with making whole foods a regular part of every day. The experience of cooking together can make a child more excited about trying new foods and more engaged during mealtime.

They develop fine motor skills. Working with their hands can help prepare toddlers for other skills, like holding a pencil or tying their shoes.

They practice patience and taking turns. Cooking involves important social skills such as waiting and sharing, especially if working with siblings and other children.

They build confidence and self-esteem. Just like the sense of accomplishment we get as adults, making food for themselves and to share with others will make toddlers beam with pride.

They hone early learning skills. Communicating with and listening to you, counting, and practicing new words during cooking are just a few ways language and math skills can be strengthened.

This book is geared toward toddlers aged two to four, but the recipes and lessons learned here can be applied to and enjoyed by all ages. All children are unique, so use your intuition when it comes to cooking with your child. Gauge your toddler's individual interest: Does your child ask to help you often? Have you had him "play" in the kitchen while you cook, or let him safely explore cooking tools or ingredients while you are preparing a meal? If so, then your toddler might be more comfortable in the kitchen and more likely to remain interested

COOKING WITH PICKY EATERS

It is completely normal and age-appropriate for toddlers to be very choosy about what they eat. New foods are scary! Our goal is to make them more familiar and, therefore, not so new anymore. Cooking is a great way to do this. By touching, smelling, chopping, stirring, and eventually tasting different foods, our kids can continue to gain the exposure they need to become increasingly familiar with those foods. **Cooking is not a magic solution for "picky eating," but it does help.** Your toddler may not want to try anything you cook together. Believe me, I've been there. It can be frustrating to get your hopes up, put in the effort to make the recipe, and then have your child turn his nose up and walk away. Your effort will eventually make a difference, though, and children are much more likely to have a healthy, fruitful relationship with food if they start participating in preparing it at a young age. **Be positive and keep trying.** If you enjoy the process together, your toddler will learn to love not only washing and chopping those veggies, but eventually eating them, too!

in following your instructions throughout the preparation of a recipe. If your child seems less interested or hesitant to cook, start slow ("Hey, cutie, want to add the milk?") and allow her to join the process at her own pace. It is completely fine if your toddler doesn't want to complete an entire recipe with you. Take a break and finish up later or do the rest yourself, then try again another day.

From a parental standpoint, it is normal to feel apprehensive about cooking with young kids. In this book, I will guide you through each step and provide the tools you need to gain confidence and lead your toddler through each recipe with ease. Young children can do so much more than we expect, and will often surprise us with their interest and ability in the kitchen if we give them the chance.

KID-FRIENDLY KITCHEN

The first step to getting your toddler safely situated in the kitchen is to find the best working space in which to cook together. There are lots of ways this can happen, and it will look different in every home, depending on your situation and comfort level. Having a "learning tower"–type step stool is nice because it allows little ones to work at counter height while being minimally monitored. Other sturdy step stools can be good, as long as you have safety rules for using them and stay with your child while he is on the stool. If you don't have an appropriate stool or feel it isn't the right option for your child, you can set up a work area at a child-size table, or even on the floor if you lay out a "splat mat" or other floor covering.

In general, you'll already have all the cooking tools you need to make the recipes in this book and will not need any specialized equipment. Some of your regular kitchen items will be particularly useful for cooking with toddlers, along with one or two kid-friendly extras.

Child-safe knife. If you only buy one tool specifically for your toddler, a serrated nylon child-safe knife would be my recommendation. This is a sturdy knife that actually cuts food but not little fingers. Search online and you will find a few good and affordable choices. To learn more about this subject, see Toddlers & Knife Safety (page 6).

Child-safe scissors. Clean scissors are a great tool for cutting herbs or other soft foods.

Measuring cups and spoons. Use the ones you already have, or buy your little chefs their own special set to get them more excited to cook.

Muffin tin and mini-muffin tin. These pans have a variety of uses, including, of course, baking muffins and cupcakes, and they're also great for presenting deconstructed salads (see page 69).

Sturdy but lightweight mixing bowls. I recommend stainless steel or plastic.

No-skid cutting boards. Try heavy wooden boards or plastic ones with a nonstick bottom. You can also make any cutting board skid-resistant by laying a damp paper towel underneath.

Box grater or handheld grater. Grating is a fun way to add extra vegetables to recipes.

Small whisk, wooden spoon, and spatula. Smaller-size tools may be easier for small hands to use.

Rolling pin. This is a fun tool, but it also teaches the fine art of pressing down "just the right amount."

Rimmed baking sheets. Line with precut parchment paper sheets or silicone mats for easy cleanup.

TODDLERS & KNIFE SAFETY

I know, toddlers and knives sounds like a recipe for disaster. Have you ever sat down at a dinner table and immediately swiped the knife away from your child's reach? I know I have. We never want our little ones to get hurt, but if you think about it, a butter knife can't cause any more harm than a pointy fork.

In fact, with the right equipment and mind-set, toddlers can learn to cut foods safely, and have the best time doing it. Handling and preparing ingredients like fresh produce exposes your child to new foods without any pressure to taste them and can be a great strategy to open picky eaters up to trying new foods. I often see my students and my own kids sneaking bites of carrots while chopping them, even though they refuse to eat them when they're on their dinner plates!

Toddlers should never use "real" adult knives, so I highly recommend buying a **child-safe nylon knife** that you can purchase online. These knives can cut through many foods but will not cut little fingers. If you don't have a child-safe knife yet, you can start by offering a butter knife to cut soft foods like bananas, zucchini, and strawberries under your supervision.

Explain that knives are tools, not toys, and that we always use any and all knives with proper form and care. That way they are prepared to safely use "real" knives in the future. Here are some tips:

- I teach my students to place their knives down flat on their cutting mats when they are not cutting food. That way there's no temptation to play with the knives or use them to goof around.

- If your child is waving the knife around, banging it on food, or not using the tool properly in any way, calmly take the knife away and direct her attention to another task such as transferring the food to a bowl or measuring another ingredient. Explain that using a knife is a big responsibility, and she can try to use it again when she shows you how to do it the proper way.

- Using a knife requires a lot of fine motor control and hand strength, so cut food into thin strips or manageably sized pieces before inviting your child to use the knife.

- Demonstrate how to hold the knife—firmly and at the top of the handle (where it meets the blade)—for good control.

- Direct your child to hold the food being cut with the other hand, with his fingers tucked under and out of the way, like a claw.

- If your toddler is getting frustrated or tired, direct her to do another task.

Citrus squeezer or handheld juicer and zester. Great for making the most of citrus fruit.

Specialized vegetable tools. Crinkle cutters, garlic press, julienne peelers, and onion/vegetable choppers are fun to use and make preparing certain vegetables easier.

Spring-loaded cookie scoops (ice cream scoops). These are great for making uniform-size cookies, filling muffin cups, or even forming meatballs. Buy a pack with three different sizes.

KITCHEN SAFETY

Safety is always the number-one priority when we have kids in the kitchen. By taking a few simple precautions, we can make the kitchen a safe place to cook and learn. That being said, **never leave a toddler unattended in the kitchen.** If you need to grab an ingredient or run to answer the door, just take your little sous chef with you.

Do safety scans. Do a quick check around your kitchen to make sure there is nothing dangerous that a child could reach up and grab: hot pan handles, sharp objects, and so on.

Be stove-safe. If anything is cooking on the stove, use rear burners whenever possible. Make sure pot or pan handles are turned to the side and away from the front of the stove. Do not push a step stool up to the stove for younger toddlers. If I want a two-year-old to help me stir at the stove, I hold him on my side, holding his outer arm with my hand, and have him place his other hand on top of my hand holding the spoon to stir. For more information on this subject, see Toddlers & Stove Safety (page 10).

Teach good lessons. Gently explain potential kitchen dangers to your child in understandable terms without being alarming. Something like "Sharp knives can give us boo-boos, so only grown-ups can use them" would work. Communication is also important when using small appliances with blades, such as blenders and food processors. Children can help as long as they know and follow the simple rules to keep them safe.

Keep sharp knives away. While you're cooking, keep sharp knives out of the vicinity. Do any prep work with your knife before you invite your child to cook with you. Alternatively, you can buy one or more of those child-safe knives I mentioned (see page 6) so you can chop side-by-side with your toddler without any fear of her grabbing a sharp knife when you turn around or her fingers getting in the way.

Respect raw eggs. Eggs can be tricky to handle, especially when toddlers want to taste everything or lick their fingers. Level 1 recipes do not involve raw eggs and are great for younger toddlers who may not understand or be able to stop themselves from eating raw ingredients. Once you feel your child is ready to handle cracking eggs, explain that eating eggs before they are cooked can make us sick. Immediately wash hands after handling raw eggs. It will become a habit and, before you know it, your child will start explaining to everyone else how to properly handle raw eggs.

COOKING TOGETHER

One more important piece of advice for cooking with toddlers: Be prepared! Here are some ways to set yourself up for cooking success:

Choose the recipe wisely. It can be helpful to have your toddler help choose the recipe to get him excited about the cooking process, but first make sure the options are appropriate for him. Look at all the recipes and

TODDLERS & STOVE SAFETY

It goes without saying that safety around heat or fire is extremely important. For that reason, there are plenty of recipes in this book that don't involve stove-top use. However, cooking at the stove top *can* be done safely with a toddler, when you and your child are ready. Use your intuition and best judgment to determine if and how your kid should participate at the stove. You know best! Some tips for safe supervised stove-top use:

* Make sure your child's hair is tied back, sleeves are rolled up, and there is no loose clothing.

* Talk to your child about remaining calm and focused on the stove: "Always keep your eyes on the spoon or the food in the pot." Looking away while stirring or adding things to a pan can cause spills and accidents.

pick two that fit the child's cooking level and interest: "We are going to be cooking breakfast together tomorrow morning. Would you like to make these French toast sticks or a baked pancake pizza?"

Review the recipe. You want to get a good feel for the recipe, the tools you will need, and the steps involved before having a child participate.

- Teach your child to keep her hands down by her sides until given directions to do otherwise.

- Don't have your child up at the stove when water is boiling or when adding ingredients to a pan on high heat, in case oil spurts or splatters.

- Turn the heat down to low or medium-low when a child adds ingredients, and hold the bowl or measuring cup together to direct his hand away from the edge of a hot pot or pan.

- Do not allow your child to hold the handle of a pot or pan, because it can be hot. Instead, instruct her to have one hand down by her side while holding the very top of the spoon or another utensil being used to stir together. Count the number of stirs you want her to do with you, then move on to the next task.

Gather your goods. Make sure all the ingredients and tools you will need to make the recipe are within reach. This will make the whole cooking process more enjoyable—pretend you're on a cooking show together!

Take your time. Make sure you have plenty of time to cook. Feeling rushed will add unnecessary stress to your cooking experience.

Set your child up for success. If the recipe has your toddler using a child-safe knife to prepare food, first cut the food into manageably sized pieces so it's easier for her to cut through the food. This usually looks like cutting food into "stick" shapes so the child can cut across the stick to

EMBRACE THE MESS

Toddlers are messy. This is not news, and there is no way around it. Give yourself a pep talk about letting go and doing your best to go with the flow. Sweeping the floor and doing a few extra dishes are well worth the numerous benefits young children gain from cooking. Some suggestions:

- Wearing an apron is exciting for little chefs and can decrease mess on clothes, but it's also okay to just go for it and change clothes after cooking.

- Keep a couple of kitchen towels handy to wipe sticky hands and clean up messes.

- Accidents happen. An egg drops onto the floor? Oopsie! Talk about the best way to clean it up. Make it fun and sing a cleanup song together. Try to have extra ingredients on hand just in case you suddenly need another egg or cup of oats.

- Gently teach ways to make less mess in the kitchen: "Hold the bowl with one hand and stir slowly with the other. We want all the flour to stay in the bowl or the cookies won't taste as good."

create a dice shape. You can cut round food in half to create a steady base, and instruct your child to always place any food being cut flat-side down for safety.

Set expectations. Toddlers often want to do everything on their own. Before you start cooking, explain what steps the child will be doing and what steps the grown-up helper will be doing. Since most toddlers understand the concept of taking turns, you can reiterate that cooking involves teamwork and that the toddler is the "chef" in charge, but all chefs have helpers in the kitchen, too.

Promote good hygiene. While you wash your hands together before cooking, talk about doing your best to keep hands clean during the cooking process. "We want to share food and toys, but not germs!" Explain that if we taste food, lick fingers, touch raw eggs, or cough/sneeze into our hands, we should wash them again.

Offer substitutions. If you are working on something that you don't want your child to taste or eat, have a snack available for him to eat instead. For example, while scooping cookie dough, I sometimes have apple slices (or a couple of chocolate chips in a little bowl) in our work area to offer my kids instead of the raw cookie dough. I also suggest having your toddler's cup or water bottle filled and ready to go.

Relax and enjoy! When it comes to teaching a love of culinary pursuits, it's important to remember that cooking is as much about the process as the end result. Take time to joke around, play, sing songs, and talk about each step or ingredient. Point out what things your child is doing well, and she will beam with pride.

Breakfast

2

There are so many fun and delicious ways to enjoy the first meal of the day. Even if you only have 10 minutes, try a colorful and nutritious Rainbow Smoothie (page 16), or make the Slow Cooker "Apple Pie" Oatmeal (page 20) together before bed to have ready and waiting for you when you wake up. For the weekend, make some cozy Pumpkin French Toast Sticks (page 27) or English Muffin Breakfast Pizzas (page 29). You'll be talking about how yummy breakfast was for the rest of the day!

Egg-free, gluten-free,
nut-free, vegetarian

Serves 2

We made this recipe on:

We enjoyed:

We rate this recipe:

☆ ☆ ☆ ☆ ☆

Recipe notes:

RAINBOW SMOOTHIE

My favorite concept to share about healthy eating in
my toddler cooking classes is "eating the rainbow."
Get your child excited about this recipe by asking his
favorite color and what fruits are that same color.
Together, lay out the rainbow of ingredients and add
them to the blender one by one. Once your child takes
a sip of the sweet, fruity drink, ask if he tastes the green
spinach. "Isn't it amazing how you made the green
spinach disappear?"

4 strawberries

½ orange or 1 small tangerine, peeled

½ banana

1 cup ice

¼ cup milk or water

¼ cup plain Greek yogurt

½ cup frozen blueberries

½ cup baby spinach (2 toddler handfuls)

1 Using a child-safe knife, remove the green
tops of the strawberries. Just for fun, chop the
strawberries smaller, chop the orange, and slice
the banana.

2 Put the ice, milk, and yogurt in the blender. Add
the banana, then the orange. Finally, add the strawberries, blueberries, and spinach.

3 Cover, then blend, and together watch what
color the drink turns. Pour into glasses and enjoy
with a fun reusable straw.

Make It Fun!

In my classes and at home, we love to do a countdown before turning on the blender: "5, 4, 3, 2, 1!" It makes the cooking process more exciting, and it also gives kids a chance to prepare for the loud blender by knowing when to cover their ears!

Level 1

Active time: 15 mins.

Egg-free, vegetarian

Serves 4

We made this recipe on:

We enjoyed:

We rate this recipe:

☆ ☆ ☆ ☆ ☆

Recipe notes:

BANANA SPLIT PARFAITS

Banana splits for breakfast? You bet! Make your morning yogurt extra special by layering it with sliced banana, a quick raspberry sauce, and crunchy granola. Get creative with the toppings and add chopped nuts, other fresh fruit, and maybe even a cherry on top! Make these in jars and store them in the fridge so you'll have a quick breakfast waiting for you in the morning. You can use gluten-free or nut-free granola, or dairy-free yogurt, to make this recipe work for any dietary needs.

2 bananas

1 cup fresh raspberries

1 teaspoon honey or maple syrup

1½ cups plain or vanilla Greek yogurt

1 cup granola

1 Using a child-safe knife, slice the bananas and set aside.

2 Put half of the raspberries in a bowl and squish them with the back of a fork to make a sauce. Stir in the honey or syrup.

3 Together, in 4 small jars or glasses, layer the banana, raspberry sauce, yogurt, granola, and remaining raspberries as desired. Top each parfait with the rest of the raspberries and enjoy immediately, or refrigerate for up to 3 days.

Technique Tip

Slicing a banana is a great first venture into using a knife and can easily be done with a butter knife. Teach your child to hold the banana with her fingers tucked under and to firmly hold the knife with the other hand.

We made this recipe on:

We enjoyed:

We rate this recipe:

☆ ☆ ☆ ☆ ☆

Recipe notes:

SLOW COOKER
"APPLE PIE" OATMEAL

Have a busy morning tomorrow? Pop all the ingredients into your slow cooker together before bedtime, and you'll have a warm and nutritious breakfast waiting for you when you wake up. With all the spices and flavors of apple pie, this dish will make it feel like you are eating dessert for breakfast. If you have whole nutmeg at home, freshly grate it for this recipe. The spice will taste even better.

1 large apple

1 cup steel-cut oats (gluten-free if desired)

2 cups milk (dairy or dairy-free)

2 cups water

3 tablespoons maple syrup, plus more for topping (optional)

1 teaspoon vanilla extract

1½ teaspoons ground cinnamon

¼ teaspoon ground nutmeg

¼ teaspoon fine salt

1 With an adult's help, hold the apple and the top of a box grater over a bowl or plate. Being careful to tuck fingers back, shred the apple on the large holes of the grater, turning the apple as you get close to the core. Transfer the grated apple and juices to a slow cooker.

2 Measure the remaining ingredients into the slow cooker and stir gently to combine.

3 Set the slow cooker on low for 8 hours. Serve warm, with an extra drizzle of maple syrup if desired.

Make It Fun!
In the morning, lay out a few different toppings to make an oatmeal toppings bar: chopped apple, chopped walnuts, hemp seeds, almond butter, honey—whatever you can dream up.

Level 2

Active time: 20 mins.
Cook time: 20 mins.

Gluten-free, nut-free

Makes 12 cups

We made this recipe on:

We enjoyed:

We rate this recipe:

☆ ☆ ☆ ☆ ☆

Recipe notes:

GREEN EGGS AND HAM CUPS

Bring out that famous Dr. Seuss book and make this a fun and delicious breakfast and activity! Spinach makes these egg muffins super green and adds a big boost of veggies to your family's morning.

6 slices deli ham

6 large eggs

2 cups baby spinach

¼ teaspoon kosher salt

Pinch freshly ground black pepper

¼ cup shredded whole or part-skim white Cheddar cheese

1 Preheat the oven to 350°F.

2 Spray a silicone muffin tray with nonstick spray, or line a regular muffin tin with paper liners and spray the liners.

3 Roll up the ham and, using a child-safe knife, chop into small pieces. Divide the chopped ham between the prepared muffin cups.

4 Crack the eggs into a bowl, then transfer them to a blender. Add the spinach, salt, and pepper to the blender.

5 Blend until smooth and very green. Together, carefully pour the egg mixture over the ham.

6 Sprinkle each muffin cup with a little cheese.

7 Bake until puffed and cooked through, about 20 minutes. Cool slightly, then remove from the cups. Serve warm.

Technique Tip

Cracking eggs is fun! I like to explain egg cracking to kids in three steps: 1. Gentle tap, tap till you hear a crack. 2. Thumbs in the crack. 3. Pull thumbs apart. (Always remind kids to hold the egg over a bowl after tapping to crack the shell—and to wash hands when they're done!)

BAKED PANCAKE "PIZZA"

This is a family favorite for good reason. It's easy: No need to use the stove to make this fun rendition of pancakes. It's interactive: Kids love topping the pancake batter however they choose. And it's fun to eat: Cut into wedges and you'll be enjoying sweet "pizza" for breakfast. Yum!

2 tablespoons butter, melted

1 large egg

½ cup milk

¼ cup unsweetened applesauce

1 tablespoon maple syrup, plus more for dipping

1 cup whole-wheat flour

1½ teaspoons baking powder

⅛ teaspoon salt

Fruit to decorate, such as sliced strawberries, sliced banana, and blueberries

1 Preheat the oven to 375°F.

2 Using a pastry brush, paint some of the melted butter onto the bottom and sides of a 10-inch cake pan. Set aside.

3 Crack the egg into a large bowl. Whisk in the remaining melted butter, the milk, applesauce, and maple syrup.

4 Add the flour, baking powder, and salt. Mix to combine. Pour the batter into the prepared pan. Top with fruit as desired.

5 Bake until a toothpick inserted in the center of the pancake comes out clean, about 18 minutes. Cool and then cut into 8 wedges. Serve with additional maple syrup for dipping.

Technique Tip

When measuring with dry measuring cups, show your child how to make the cups "full and flat." Teach your toddler how to use a butter knife to level off the top of the cup and to never pack dry ingredients when measuring unless directed.

PUMPKIN FRENCH TOAST STICKS

Level 2

Active time: 15 mins.
Cook time: 15 mins.

Nut-free, vegetarian

Serves 4

Pumpkin is one of my family's favorite breakfast flavors. Baking the French toast instead of cooking it on the stove top makes this recipe more toddler-friendly and allows you to do something else while breakfast is in the oven. Plus, the sticks are so fun to eat! Dip them in maple syrup, yogurt, or applesauce. Thicker slices of bread work best, but you can use any type of bread you like. Don't have pumpkin pie spice at home? Make your own by mixing together 3 tablespoons ground cinnamon, 2 teaspoons ground ginger, 1 teaspoon ground nutmeg, 1 teaspoon ground allspice, and ½ teaspoon ground cloves.

1 tablespoon melted butter or vegetable oil

4 or 5 slices whole-wheat bread

2 large eggs

¼ cup milk

¼ cup canned pumpkin purée

1 teaspoon maple syrup, plus more for dipping

½ teaspoon pumpkin pie spice or ground cinnamon

½ teaspoon vanilla extract

We made this recipe on:

We enjoyed:

We rate this recipe:

☆ ☆ ☆ ☆ ☆

Recipe notes:

1 Preheat the oven to 375°F.

2 Line a baking sheet with parchment paper or aluminum foil and grease with the butter or oil.

3 Using a child-safe knife, cut each slice of bread into three sticks. Remove the side crusts if desired.

There's more

4 Crack the eggs into a large bowl or pie pan. Add the milk, pumpkin, maple syrup, spice, and vanilla, and whisk together to combine.

5 Working with two or three pieces at a time, dip the bread into the egg mixture, allowing the bread to soak up the liquid for at least 10 to 15 seconds per side. (Have a towel nearby to wipe off little hands!) Once both sides of the bread have been dipped, allow the excess to drip off, then place the bread on the prepared baking sheet. Repeat with the remaining bread pieces.

6 Bake until the bread is lightly browned and crunchy on the outside, 14 to 16 minutes. Serve with maple syrup for dipping.

7 Freeze any leftovers in a single layer until solid, then place in a container or freezer bag for up to a month. Reheat in the oven at 375°F until warmed through, about 10 minutes.

MMMM...
PUMPKIN PIE
FOR BREAKFAST!

Make It Fun!
Explore spices! Show your child that spices don't mean spicy hot. Smell different yummy spices found in your kitchen, like cinnamon, ginger, cumin, and coriander, and talk about what they remind you of.

ENGLISH MUFFIN BREAKFAST PIZZAS

What's more fun than having pizza for breakfast? Get creative with the egg scramble part of this dish and add whatever vegetables you like, such as spinach, broccoli, or tomatoes. Cooking eggs is a great skill to learn (see page 10 for more tips on cooking safely with toddlers at the stove).

2 whole-wheat English muffins

½ red bell pepper, seeds and ribs removed

1 link cooked chicken sausage

2 large eggs

1 teaspoon extra-virgin olive oil

2 tablespoons cream cheese

½ cup shredded whole or part-skim mozzarella cheese

1 Preheat the oven to 400°F. Split and toast the English muffins. Set them on a baking sheet lined with parchment paper or aluminum foil.

2 Cut the pepper into strips and halve the sausage lengthwise.

3 Using a child-safe knife, chop the pepper into a small dice. Place the sausage flat-side down on a cutting board and cut into bite-size pieces.

4 Crack the eggs into a small bowl and whisk with a fork.

There's more

Active time: 20 mins.
Cook time: 7 mins.

Nut-free

Serves 2

We made this recipe on:

We enjoyed:

We rate this recipe:

☆ ☆ ☆ ☆ ☆

Recipe notes:

5 In a small nonstick pan over medium heat, heat the oil. Together, add the chopped pepper and sausage. Stir to heat. Add the eggs. Turn the heat to low and cook, stirring occasionally, until cooked through, 1 to 2 minutes. Transfer the cooked egg mixture to a bowl and set aside to cool.

6 While the egg is cooking, spread the English muffin halves with the cream cheese.

7 Spoon the warm scrambled egg mixture onto the English muffins, dividing evenly among the four halves. Sprinkle some of the cheese on top of each muffin.

8 Bake the breakfast pizzas until the cheese is melted, about 5 minutes. Serve warm.

Technique Tip

Many of us learned to tap an egg on the side of a bowl to start the cracking process. However, the safest way to crack the shell is by gently tapping it on a flat surface, like a table. Less shell will get into the bowl, and your little chef will be less likely to accidentally crack the egg too hard and spill it everywhere.

SWEET POTATO HASH BROWN WAFFLES

I love experimenting with new ways to use the waffle iron. This recipe couldn't be easier or more delicious. Serve the crispy sweet potatoes with some sliced avocado, salsa, or a sunny-side-up egg.

1 medium sweet potato

2 teaspoons vegetable oil, plus more for greasing the waffle iron

2 large eggs

1 tablespoon cornstarch or potato starch

¼ teaspoon garlic powder

¼ teaspoon kosher salt

⅛ teaspoon paprika

⅛ teaspoon ground cumin (optional)

1 With an adult's help, peel the sweet potato and grate on the large holes of a box grater. Measure 2 heaping cups of grated potato.

2 Heat the waffle iron and grease well with oil.

3 Crack the eggs into a large bowl. Add the grated sweet potato and the remaining ingredients, and stir to combine.

4 Scoop ½ cup of the sweet potato mixture into the center of the waffle iron. Place a kitchen towel on top of the iron and carefully press down. Cook the waffle until golden brown, 4 to 5 minutes. Once the waffle is ready, gently remove with a butter knife and transfer to a plate. Repeat with the remaining mixture.

Technique Tip
If you don't have a waffle maker, you can panfry this mixture in little patties to make sweet potato fritters. Buy some frozen pre-shredded potatoes if you want to make this recipe even easier.

Lunch

Have some midday fun by making cozy soup or creamy pasta to enjoy together. You can cook up some of these recipes ahead of time, like Broccoli Nuggets (page 43) or Sandwich "Sushi" Rolls (page 50), to pack in a lunch box for school or an outing away from home. Whether your little one is eating at home or on the road, these lunch recipes are easy to make and fun to eat!

3

Level 1

Active time: 15 mins.
Cook time: 5 mins.

Egg-free, gluten-free,
nut-free, vegetarian

Serves 4

We made this recipe on:

We enjoyed:

We rate this recipe:

☆ ☆ ☆ ☆ ☆

Recipe notes:

SUPER EASY TOMATO SOUP

This soup couldn't be easier to make: Add everything to a blender, blend, then heat and enjoy! Serve it with a classic grilled cheese or some crackers for a quick and delicious lunch. I like to add a few handfuls of spinach to get in an extra serving of veggies. Once the soup is blended together, you can hardly notice any greens in there.

1 (28-ounce) can whole or crushed tomatoes with basil

½ cup milk or water

½ teaspoon garlic powder

1 to 2 packed cups baby spinach

½ teaspoon kosher salt

2 tablespoons sour cream or plain yogurt

½ teaspoon honey (optional)

Shredded Parmesan or whole or part-skim mozzarella cheese, for serving (optional)

1 Measure all the ingredients except the cheese, then transfer them to a blender.

2 Cover the blender, do a countdown together, then have your child help you turn on the blender. Blend the ingredients until smooth.

3 Pour the soup into a small pot and heat over low heat until warm, about 5 minutes. Ladle into bowls.

4 Sprinkle with cheese if desired.

Heads Up

Although the veggies "disap-pear" into the sauce, you are not hiding them, because you put them in there together. Kids can't learn to like foods if they don't know they've tried them! Cooking together is a great way to introduce new foods.

PIZZA TOASTS WITH "DISAPPEARING" VEGGIE SAUCE

Level 1

Active time: 15 mins.
Cook time: 5 mins.

Egg-free, nut-free, vegetarian

Serves 2

Adding chopped or grated vegetables to tomato sauce is one of the best ways to introduce more vegetables into a veggie skeptic's life.

4 slices whole-wheat bread

1 carrot

¼ cup raw or cooked broccoli florets

½ cup marinara or pizza sauce

1 cup shredded whole or part-skim mozzarella cheese

Turkey pepperoni, chopped bell pepper, and/or olives, for topping (optional)

We made this recipe on:

We enjoyed:

1 Preheat the oven to 400°F. Lightly toast the bread slices in a toaster.

2 Cut the toasts into shapes with a cookie cutter if desired. Place on a baking tray.

3 With an adult's help, peel the carrot, then grate it on the smaller holes of a box grater. Use a child-safe knife to finely chop the tops of the broccoli florets, reserving the rest for use in another recipe. In a medium bowl, combine the grated carrot, broccoli, and marinara sauce and stir to mix.

We rate this recipe:

☆ ☆ ☆ ☆ ☆

Recipe notes:

4 Spoon some sauce over each piece of toast and spread it around with the back of the spoon. Sprinkle the cheese over the toasts and add any toppings as desired.

5 Bake the toasts until the cheese is melted, about 5 minutes. Serve warm.

SMASHED-BEAN QUESADILLAS WITH EASY SALSA DIP

Another great use for that potato masher? Mashing cooked beans! This lunch is quick and full of flavor. The assembled quesadillas are oven-baked to crisp the tortillas and melt the cheese, giving your little one time to mix up the quick dip to go alongside. If you have time, why not cut up a few crunchy veggies to dip in there as well?

1 (14-ounce) can pinto or black beans, drained and rinsed

½ teaspoon chili powder

¼ teaspoon garlic powder

Pinch salt

1 to 2 tablespoons vegetable oil

4 (8- to 10-inch) whole-wheat tortillas

1 cup shredded whole or part-skim Cheddar cheese or Mexican cheese blend, divided

½ cup jarred mild salsa

½ cup plain Greek yogurt

1 Preheat the oven to 400°F. Line a baking sheet with parchment paper or aluminum foil.

2 Place the beans in a large bowl and mash with a potato masher or the back of a fork. Stir in the chili powder, garlic powder, and a big pinch of salt. Set aside.

There's more ➡️

Level 1

Active time: 20 mins.
Cook time: 10 mins.

Egg-free, nut-free, vegetarian

Serves 2

We made this recipe on:

We enjoyed:

We rate this recipe:
☆☆☆☆☆

Recipe notes:

3 Use a pastry brush to paint a little oil all over one side of 2 tortillas. Place them oiled-side down on the prepared baking sheet. Sprinkle about ¼ cup of shredded cheese over each tortilla. Add the mashed beans on top of the cheese, then divide the remaining ½ cup cheese on top of the beans. Place the remaining 2 tortillas on top and press down gently. Paint a little oil over the top tortillas.

4 Bake until the tortillas are golden brown and the cheese is melted, about 10 minutes.

5 While the quesadillas are cooking, stir the salsa and yogurt together in a small bowl.

6 Let the quesadillas cool in the pan, then cut into wedges. Serve with the dipping sauce.

Heads Up
Young kids get really excited about painting with oil. Instruct your little one to only dip the brush in the oil once while painting a side of a tortilla, or you might get more oil on the quesadilla than you bargained for.

BROCCOLI NUGGETS

Broccoli is the star of this dippable, kid-friendly recipe. These veggie nuggets are great served as a side dish or in a lunch box, and they can be made ahead and stored in the freezer to pull out and reheat for a quick meal. We love this recipe at my house for so many reasons, but mostly because it's so fun to make. Using a silicone muffin tin is recommended, but if you don't have one, just grease your metal pan very well to prevent sticking.

Vegetable oil, for greasing

4 cups small broccoli florets (about 1 medium head of broccoli)

1 cup cooked quinoa or 1¼ cups cooked brown or white rice, cooled

1 large egg

¼ cup finely shredded whole or part-skim Cheddar or mozzarella cheese, plus more to sprinkle on top

¼ teaspoon garlic powder

¼ teaspoon kosher salt

Ranch dressing, ketchup, or your favorite dipping sauce

Level 2

Active time: 20 mins.
Cook time: 12 mins.

Gluten-free, nut-free, vegetarian

Makes 24 nuggets

We made this recipe on:

We enjoyed:

We rate this recipe:

☆ ☆ ☆ ☆ ☆

Recipe notes:

1. Preheat the oven to 400°F.

2. Brush a 24-cup mini-muffin tin with oil.

3. With an adult's help and supervision, place the broccoli florets in a food processor, cover, and pulse until finely chopped. Add the quinoa or rice, egg, cheese, garlic powder, and salt. Continue to pulse until all the ingredients are combined and uniform in size.

There's more

4. Remove the blade from the food processor and set aside, out of reach of little hands.

5. Spoon about a tablespoon of the broccoli mixture into each muffin cup, then use the back of the spoon or fingers to pack the mixture down. Sprinkle the top of each "nugget" with a little extra cheese if desired.

6. Bake until lightly browned around the edges, 10 to 12 minutes. Allow the nuggets to cool completely. You may need to loosen the edges with a butter knife to help remove them from the pan. Enjoy with your favorite dipping sauce.

Technique Tip

Have your kids crack the eggs into a separate bowl before adding them to a recipe. You don't want to be fishing shells out of a food processor or blender!

Level 1

Active time: 15 mins.

Gluten-free, vegan

Serves 2

We made this recipe on:

We enjoyed:

We rate this recipe:

☆ ☆ ☆ ☆ ☆

Recipe notes:

GREEN MONSTER SMOOTHIE BOWLS

Smoothie bowls might not be the most conventional lunch, but when you blend fruit, veggies, and almond butter and add on some fun toppings, you get a nutritious, filling, and interactive meal. Encourage your little one to make a silly face with the toppings, and you'll be pleasantly surprised when he asks for more. Cauliflower might seem like an unusual thing to put in a smoothie, but it adds nutrients without any taste at all.

1 frozen sliced banana

1 cup frozen mango or pineapple

2 cups baby spinach or chopped kale leaves

½ cup frozen cauliflower "rice" (optional)

2 tablespoons almond butter

½ cup coconut milk, almond milk, or any milk of your choice, plus more if needed

Additional toppings: sliced banana or other fruit, granola, and/or chopped nuts

1 Put all the ingredients except the additional toppings in a blender.

2 Cover and blend until smooth and thick like ice cream. Add a little more milk if necessary. Pour or scoop the smoothie into bowls.

3 Top the smoothie bowl as desired, with sliced banana or other fruit, granola, and/or chopped nuts, to make a crazy monster face or a happy face, and enjoy!

Technique Tip

When measuring liquids, teach your kid to place the liquid measuring cup on a flat surface, pour the liquid just under the line, then lower her head to eye level to check that the liquid is at the accurate measurement line.

CREAMY MAC AND PEAS

Pasta with peas is my older son Jack's favorite comfort food. This easy, cheesy sauce comes together in just a few minutes. Whipped cream cheese is easier to mix into cooked pasta, but you can also use regular softened cream cheese for this dish. Experiment with different kinds of pasta. I love using pasta made from chickpeas or lentils because it is higher in protein and fiber. Don't have peas? Add some chopped broccoli instead and call it Mac and Trees!

2 cups small shaped pasta

1 tablespoon butter

3 tablespoons whipped cream cheese

1 cup peas (thawed if frozen)

⅛ teaspoon kosher salt

⅛ teaspoon garlic powder (optional)

1 tablespoon grated Parmesan cheese (optional)

1 Cook the pasta in salted boiling water according to the package directions, 8 to 12 minutes, depending on the pasta being used.

2 While the pasta is cooking, cut the butter into pea-size pieces. Put in a large bowl and add the cream cheese and peas.

3 Drain the pasta and add to the bowl with the cream cheese.

4 Once the pasta has stopped steaming a lot, sprinkle with the salt and garlic powder (if using). Carefully stir the pasta until it is coated with the creamy sauce. Serve warm, sprinkled with Parmesan cheese if desired.

Level 2

Active time: 15 mins.

Nut-free, vegan

Serves 2

We made this recipe on:

We enjoyed:

We rate this recipe:

☆ ☆ ☆ ☆ ☆

Recipe notes:

SANDWICH "SUSHI" ROLLS

Kids have the best time using a rolling pin to put this unique spin on a sandwich. You can stuff it with whatever you like: nut butter and jelly, turkey and cheese, or veggies like this California roll–inspired filling.

4 slices whole-wheat bread

1 small English cucumber (or peeled slicing cucumber)

½ avocado, pit removed

¼ cup hummus

¼ cup grated or shredded carrot

1 Cut the crusts off the bread.

2 Using a child-safe knife, slice the cucumber into rounds, then cut each round across into 3 or 4 strips. Cut the avocado into 8 slices.

3 Use a rolling pin to flatten each slice of bread; get it as thin as possible without tearing it.

4 Spread a thin layer of hummus over each slice of flattened bread. In the center of each bread slice, place a few slices of cucumber, 2 slices of avocado, and a sprinkle of grated carrot. Starting with the longer side of each bread slice, roll the edge over the fillings, then continue to roll until the bread meets and seals.

5 Cut each roll into 6 to 8 pieces and serve.

Technique Tip

Spreading can be a tricky activity for little hands, and it takes practice. Use a small or kid-size butter knife if you have one, and hold the knife with your child to help demonstrate the motion you use for spreading something on the bread.

Level 3

Active time: 20 mins.

Dairy-free, egg-free, gluten-free

Serves 2

We made this recipe on:

We enjoyed:

We rate this recipe:

☆ ☆ ☆ ☆ ☆

Recipe notes:

CHICKEN BLT KEBABS

We have a saying at home and in my classes: "Everything is better on a stick!" Feel free to add toasted bread or other veggies to customize your own sandwich sticks. If you are worried about the sharp points on the wooden skewers, use paper lollipop sticks or cocktail straws instead.

1 cup grape tomatoes
4 or 5 large romaine lettuce leaves
½ English cucumber
1 baked or grilled chicken breast
4 strips cooked bacon
1 teaspoon Dijon mustard
½ teaspoon honey
1 tablespoon balsamic vinegar
2 tablespoons extra-virgin olive oil
Salt
Freshly ground black pepper

1 Using a child-safe knife, cut the tomatoes into halves. Cut the lettuce, cucumber, chicken, and bacon into bite-size pieces.

2 Carefully thread one piece each of tomato, lettuce, cucumber, chicken, and bacon onto a skewer, then repeat the pattern one more time. Assemble three more kebabs with the remaining ingredients.

3 In a small bowl, whisk the mustard, honey, vinegar, and oil until combined. Season with salt and pepper to taste. Drizzle the dressing over the kebabs or serve on the side for dipping.

Technique Tip

Cutting round food like tomatoes can be tricky. You can teach kids to pinch a small tomato between their thumb and pointer finger, carefully place the tip of the (child-safe) knife through the little bridge made by the two fingers, and then saw the knife back and forth to cut.

Dinner

I believe in one dinner for the whole family! C'mon, get your toddler on board with this plan by cooking the meal together. From my cozy Chicken Parm Pasta Bake (page 57) to fun assemble-your-own Roasted Shrimp and Veggie Sushi Rice Bowls (page 83), we've got inventive choices to make dinnertime delicious. Remember that you don't have to cook dinner together in the evening. Feel free to make part of your meal in the morning, after lunch, or whenever you have a bit of free time. This will give you a great daytime activity and take some pressure off the before-dinner rush.

Falafel Burgers with Lemony
Yogurt Sauce, page 65

CHICKEN PARM PASTA BAKE

Here's classic comfort food that you can easily make together at home! Customize this recipe by adding broccoli, grated zucchini, chopped bell pepper, or any other vegetables you and your little one like. This dish is easy to make ahead and have waiting in the fridge to pop into the oven later in the day. You can also double the recipe and freeze half for dinner another night. I usually use store-bought rotisserie chicken or leftover roast chicken for this dish, but any cooked chicken will work well.

12 ounces whole-wheat fusilli or penne pasta (or any kind of pasta)

1 tablespoon extra-virgin olive oil, plus more for greasing

1 carrot

2 cups baby spinach (optional)

1 (24-ounce) jar marinara sauce

2 cups cooked chicken

2 cups shredded whole or part-skim mozzarella cheese, divided

½ cup panko bread crumbs

¼ cup grated Parmesan cheese

1 Cook the pasta in salted boiling water according to the package directions. Drain and set aside.

2 Preheat the oven to 425°F. Together, grease a 9-by-13-inch baking dish with olive oil.

Active time: 20 mins.
Cook time: 20 mins.

Egg-free, nut-free

Serves 4

We made this recipe on:

We enjoyed:

We rate this recipe:
☆ ☆ ☆ ☆ ☆

Recipe notes:

There's more

3 With an adult's help, peel the carrot. Hold a grater and carrot together and shred the carrot to yield about ½ cup finely grated carrot. Put in a large bowl. Tear the spinach (if using) into smaller pieces and add to the bowl with the carrot. Pour the marinara sauce over the vegetables in the bowl and stir to combine.

4 Shred the cooked chicken with your hands or use a child-safe knife to chop it into small pieces. Add to the bowl with the veggies and sauce. Add the cooked pasta and 1 cup of shredded mozzarella.

5 Together, stir the pasta and sauce, then transfer to the prepared pan and spread into an even layer.

6 In a separate bowl, mix the remaining 1 cup shredded mozzarella, the panko, grated Parmesan cheese, and olive oil. Sprinkle over the top of the pasta in the baking dish.

7 Bake until the top is golden brown and the cheese is melted, 10 to 15 minutes. Serve warm.

Technique Tip

Kitchen gadgets are often necessary and can be fun to use, but don't forget that little hands are also wonderfully versatile tools. Sprinkle, rip, shred, pull apart—there are so many ways our hands can help us cook!

RAINBOW RICE NOODLES WITH ROASTED TOFU

I've found that kids get excited about making any recipe with "rainbow" in the title. We can talk about what colors we eat and how they keep our bodies strong and healthy, as well as how "eating the rainbow" is delicious and fun. If your family doesn't like the vegetables suggested here, go ahead and substitute your faves. If you prefer cooked veggies in your noodles, you can sauté vegetables like peppers and broccoli beforehand (or roast 'em alongside the tofu). Also, feel free to leave out the tofu or substitute cooked chicken or shrimp.

1 (14-ounce) package extra-firm tofu

1 teaspoon vegetable oil

½ red bell pepper, ribs and seeds removed

½ yellow bell pepper, ribs and seeds removed

1 carrot

½ English cucumber, halved lengthwise

½ cup shredded red cabbage

1 (8-ounce) package thin or thick rice noodles, cooked according to package directions

¼ cup peanut butter, almond butter, or tahini

¼ cup low-sodium soy sauce or tamari

2 tablespoons rice vinegar

1 tablespoon honey or agave syrup

1 tablespoon toasted sesame seeds

Level 1

Active time: 20 mins.
Cook time: 15 mins.

Gluten-free, vegan

Serves 4

We made this recipe on:

We enjoyed:

We rate this recipe:

☆ ☆ ☆ ☆ ☆

Recipe notes:

There's more

1. Preheat the oven to 425°F. Line a baking sheet with parchment paper or nonstick aluminum foil.

2. Drain the tofu and pat dry with paper towels. Cut into ½-inch-thick slices.

3. Using a child-safe knife, cut the tofu into ½-inch cubes. Put in a medium bowl and drizzle with the oil. Toss with hands to coat the tofu in the oil. Dump the tofu onto the lined baking sheet and spread the cubes out in a single layer so they aren't touching.

4. Roast the tofu until golden brown around the edges, about 15 minutes. Set aside to cool, then transfer to a bowl.

5. While the tofu cooks, prepare the vegetables. Slice the bell peppers. With help from an adult, peel and shred the carrot on a box grater. Slice the cucumber and finely chop the cabbage. Place all the vegetables in a large bowl. Add the cooked noodles on top.

6. To make the sauce, whisk the peanut butter, soy sauce, rice vinegar, and honey together in a small bowl. Pour the sauce over the noodles and add the tofu. Toss with tongs until all the ingredients are coated in the sauce. Serve at room temperature or cold, sprinkled with the sesame seeds.

AUTUMN VEGGIE, APPLE, AND SAUSAGE SHEET PAN SUPPER

Level 1

Active time: 15 mins.
Cook time: 30 mins.

Dairy-free, egg-free,
gluten-free, nut-free

Serves 4

Sheet pan dinners are made by cooking everything for a meal on one pan in the oven. These are very popular for good reason: They are easy to assemble, quick to clean up, and delicious! This recipe contains some vegetables that are a little tougher for kid-safe knives to get through, but there are still a lot of other ways for children to participate. If you like, you can cut those tougher vegetables ahead of time, then have your little chef do the other steps.

½ pound peeled butternut squash

12 ounces cooked chicken or turkey sausage, such as smoked turkey kielbasa, cut in half lengthwise

2 crisp baking apples, such as Honeycrisp, cored and cut into 12 slices

1 medium sweet potato, peeled and cut into ½-inch cubes

8 ounces Brussels sprouts, halved or quartered

2 garlic cloves

¼ cup extra-virgin olive oil

4 sprigs fresh thyme or 1 teaspoon dried thyme

Coarse sea salt or kosher salt

Freshly ground black pepper

1. Preheat the oven to 400°F. Line 2 baking sheets with parchment paper or spray with nonstick cooking spray.

2. Cut the butternut squash into ¼-inch sticks.

We made this recipe on:

We enjoyed:

We rate this recipe:
☆ ☆ ☆ ☆ ☆

Recipe notes:

There's more ➡

3 Using a child-safe knife, cut the butternut squash sticks into cubes. Slice the sausage in half length-wise. Cut each apple slice into 3 chunks. Put the squash, sausage, and apples in a large bowl, and add the sweet potato and Brussels sprouts.

4 Crush the garlic cloves in a garlic press or mince with a child-safe knife. Add the garlic and olive oil to the large bowl with the sausage. Pick the fresh thyme leaves off the stem and add those to the bowl, along with a big pinch of salt and a few grinds of black pepper. Toss everything together with a large spoon or hands. Transfer the mixture to the prepared pan and spread out evenly.

5 Roast until the vegetables are golden brown and tender, 25 to 30 minutes. Serve warm.

Technique Tip

When cutting through harder foods with a child-safe knife, instruct your child to place her free hand (the hand not holding the knife) on top of the knife and press down. We call this the "top chop."

FALAFEL BURGERS WITH LEMONY YOGURT SAUCE

I love pairing more unfamiliar foods like beans or veggies with fun and more familiar concepts like burgers. Veggie burgers don't have to be bland or boring—experiment with flavorful spices such as cumin or coriander, and add yummy toppings such as sliced tomatoes, avocado, or cucumber. If you make the burger patties even smaller, you can serve them as "nuggets," without a bun, and with the sauce (or ketchup) on the side for dipping.

¼ red onion, cut into chunks

1 medium carrot, peeled and cut into chunks

½ cup fresh parsley or cilantro leaves

½ cup rolled oats

½ teaspoon garlic powder, divided

½ teaspoon kosher salt, plus more for seasoning

¼ teaspoon baking powder

1 (14-ounce) can chickpeas, drained and rinsed

1 tablespoon extra-virgin olive oil

3 tablespoons freshly squeezed lemon juice (1 to 2 lemons), divided

1 cup plain Greek yogurt

6 small hamburger buns, toasted

Level 1

Active time: 20 mins.
Cook time: 20 mins.

Egg-free, nut-free, vegetarian

Makes 6 small burgers

We made this recipe on:

We enjoyed:

We rate this recipe:

☆ ☆ ☆ ☆ ☆

Recipe notes:

1 Preheat the oven to 400°F. Line a baking sheet with parchment paper or aluminum foil.

There's more

2 Put the onion, carrot, parsley, oats, ¼ teaspoon garlic powder, the salt, and baking powder in the bowl of a food processor.

3 Cover the food processor and have your child pulse until everything is finely chopped. Together, add the chickpeas, oil, and 1 tablespoon of lemon juice, then cover and pulse again until roughly chopped.

4 Remove the blade from the food processor, placing it out of reach, and dump the mixture into a bowl. Pat the mixture down, then use your hands to score and divide it into 6 sections. Together, roll the sections into balls, then pat them into patties. Place on the prepared baking sheet. Bake until golden brown around the edges, about 20 minutes. Set aside to cool.

5 While the burgers are baking, mix the yogurt with the remaining ¼ teaspoon garlic powder, the remaining 2 tablespoons of lemon juice, and a big pinch of salt. Serve the burgers warm on the toasted buns with sauce on top or on the side.

Heads Up

Chopping onion in the food processor might irritate little eyes. Make sure your toddler doesn't put her face directly over the bowl.

MUFFIN TIN COBB SALAD WITH RASPBERRY DRESSING

Level 2

Active time: 30 mins.
Cook time: 15 mins.

Dairy-free, gluten-free, nut-free

Serves 4

We don't usually think of salads as typical toddler fare. However, if we "deconstruct" the meal and serve it in a fun way, kids can enjoy the different components of the salad and pick out which parts they'd like to eat. Serving meals or snacks in a muffin tin, "salad bar–style," also adds an element of novelty, which can help little ones get more excited about mealtime. There are lots of ways to customize this salad recipe: Replace the bacon with cooked chicken or shrimp, or add different vegetables like corn and cucumbers.

8 strips thick-cut bacon

1 avocado, halved, pitted, peeled, and cut into quarters

2 plum tomatoes, cut into quarters

1 romaine heart, stem end removed

4 hard-boiled large eggs, peeled

¼ cup fresh raspberries

1 teaspoon Dijon mustard

1 teaspoon maple syrup or honey

2 tablespoons apple cider vinegar

6 tablespoons extra-virgin olive oil

Salt

Freshly ground black pepper

We made this recipe on:

We enjoyed:

We rate this recipe:

☆ ☆ ☆ ☆ ☆

Recipe notes:

There's more ➡

1 Preheat the oven to 400°F. Line a baking sheet with aluminum foil. Your child can help you lay the bacon out on the pan in a single layer. Wash hands. Bake until cooked to your liking, about 15 minutes. Transfer the cooked bacon to a plate lined with paper towels.

2 Using a child-safe knife, cut the avocado into bite-size pieces and place in a small bowl. Repeat with the tomatoes and place in another small bowl. Rip or cut the lettuce into bite-size pieces. Cut the eggs into quarters. Once the bacon is cooled, use a knife or scissors to cut it into bite-size pieces.

3 In a small bowl, mash the raspberries with the back of a fork until completely broken up. Whisk in the mustard, maple syrup, and vinegar. Slowly incorporate the oil and whisk to combine, then season with a pinch of salt and pepper to taste.

4 Place each salad component in a different hole of a muffin tin to be assembled as desired, with the dressing on the side for dipping.

LETTUCE EAT!

BREAKFAST-FOR-DINNER FRIED RICE

Level 2

Active time: 15 mins.
Cook time: 10 mins.

Dairy-free, gluten-free, nut-free

Serves 4

It's always fun to change things up and have breakfast for dinner once in a while! Fried rice is one of my family's favorite quick meals, and I love how versatile it is. Use leftover cooked rice or buy precooked rice from the store to make this dinner come together in no time. You can include whatever veggies you have at home or whatever protein your family likes best, such as diced ham, bacon, or even chicken. If you like, instead of scrambling the eggs into the rice, serve an over-easy egg on top of everyone's individual plate.

1 carrot, peeled and cut into ¼-inch sticks

4 links cooked chicken or turkey breakfast sausage, cut in half lengthwise

1 tablespoon sesame oil or vegetable oil

4 large eggs

2 tablespoons low-sodium soy sauce or tamari

1 teaspoon rice vinegar

¼ teaspoon garlic powder

4 scallions, trimmed and thinly sliced, green and white parts separated

1 cup frozen peas

5 cups cooked rice, at room temperature

Toasted sesame seeds (optional)

1 Using a child-safe knife, chop the carrot into a small dice. Set aside. Cut the sausage into bite-size pieces. Set aside.

We made this recipe on:

We enjoyed:

We rate this recipe:
☆ ☆ ☆ ☆ ☆

Recipe notes:

There's more ➡

2 In a large skillet over medium-high heat, heat the oil. Add the carrot and sausage. Cook until lightly browned, about 1 minute.

3 Meanwhile, crack the eggs into a large bowl and whisk together. In a small bowl, mix the soy sauce, vinegar, and garlic powder. Set aside. Together, add the scallion whites and peas to the pan and cook, stirring occasionally, for 1 minute.

4 Move everything over to one side of the pan, then pour the eggs into the empty side. Use a spatula to scramble the eggs. Once the eggs are fully cooked, add the rice. Cook until warmed through, about 1 minute, then pour the sauce over the top. Stir together until well mixed.

5 Garnish with the scallion greens and a sprinkle of sesame seeds if desired.

Heads Up

There is some time up at the stove for this recipe, so make sure your toddler knows ahead of time what his role will be while up at the pan. Will he help stir once in a while and then watch? Where will he put his hands while helping or while watching?

Make It Fun!
This easy pasta recipe has lots of spring vegetables and flavors, so it's a great opportunity to talk about seasons and what kinds of foods grow during that time of year.

SUPER GREEN SPAGHETTI

At home and in my classes, I love to create color-themed meals and dishes as a way to have fun with fresh fruits and vegetables. To get excited about the green theme in your kitchen, talk about all the different green foods you could find at the grocery store or farmers' market. Even better, take a trip to the store together and have your little ones choose one or two green vegetables that they'd like to include in this yummy spaghetti recipe. Use gluten-free spaghetti if you wish, and leave out the Parmesan cheese if you want to make this dish dairy-free.

1 pound spinach (green) spaghetti or any other spaghetti of choice

2 cups broccoli florets (about 1 small head)

½ bunch asparagus

1 small zucchini

2 cups sugar snap peas, trimmed

2 garlic cloves

1 lemon

3 tablespoons extra-virgin olive oil

¼ cup fresh basil leaves, plus more for serving (optional)

Salt

Freshly ground black pepper

Grated Parmesan cheese, for serving (optional)

1. Cook the pasta in salted boiling water as directed on the package. Drain, reserving ½ cup of the cooking water. Set aside.

There's more

Level 3

Active time: 25 mins.
Cook time: 15 mins.

Nut-free, vegan

Serves 4

We made this recipe on:

We enjoyed:

We rate this recipe:
☆☆☆☆☆

Recipe notes:

2 Using a child-safe knife, chop the broccoli into small pieces. Snap the ends off the asparagus, then cut the stalks into small rounds. Cut the ends off the zucchini, then cut into a small dice. Cut the snap peas into 3 or 4 pieces. Place all the vegetables in a large bowl.

3 Together, mince, grate, or use a garlic press to crush the garlic. Zest the lemon, holding a Microplane or another small zester together. Cut the lemon in half, then juice it into a small bowl.

4 In a large sauté pan over medium heat, heat the oil.

5 Together, carefully add the chopped vegetables to the pan. Give a slow stir with a wooden spoon. While the vegetables cook, rip up the fresh basil and set aside.

6 Together, stir the garlic into the pan and cook for 30 seconds. Add the lemon zest and juice. Together, add the reserved ½ cup of pasta water and simmer for 1 minute to evaporate some of the liquid.

7 Turn off the heat, then add the cooked spaghetti to the pan. Stir to incorporate the vegetables and pasta. Add additional water to thin the sauce as needed. Taste for seasoning and add salt and pepper as needed. Kids can sprinkle on some cheese or additional basil if desired.

EASY ALPHABET SOUP

This recipe is one of my son Jack's favorite meals. He loves to help chop the vegetables, and he gets so excited to find all the letters in his name while eating the fun pasta in the soup. Using jarred marinara in this recipe adds a ton of flavor without a lot of work. Cooked pasta will absorb lots of liquid if left in the soup for an extended period of time. So instead of adding all the pasta to the liquid, pour soup into individual bowls and then add the desired amount of pasta directly into each bowl. This way leftover pasta can be saved separately.

1 large carrot, peeled and cut into ½-inch sticks

1 celery stalk, trimmed and cut into ½-inch sticks

¼ pound (about 2 cups) green beans, trimmed

1 tablespoon extra-virgin olive oil

½ large onion, finely chopped

½ teaspoon kosher salt, plus more if needed

1 cup jarred marinara sauce

3 cups vegetable broth or water

1 cup frozen peas, frozen corn, or a combination

1 cup alphabet-shaped pasta (or any other small-shaped pasta), cooked according to package directions

¼ cup grated Parmesan cheese (optional)

1 Together, use a child-safe knife to cut the carrot, celery, and green beans into small pieces. Put the carrot and celery in a small bowl, keeping the green beans separate.

There's more ➡️

We made this recipe on:

We enjoyed:

We rate this recipe:
☆ ☆ ☆ ☆ ☆

Recipe notes:

2　In a large soup pot or Dutch oven over medium heat, heat the oil. Assist your child in carefully adding the onion, carrot, celery, and salt. Cook, stirring occasionally, until the vegetables have softened slightly, about 5 minutes.

3　Together, add the marinara sauce, broth or water, and green beans. Holding the top of a long-handled spoon with your toddler, carefully stir. Bring the pot to a simmer and cook until the vegetables are tender, about 10 minutes. Stir in the frozen vegetables. Turn off the heat and taste for seasoning, adding more salt as needed. Ladle the soup into bowls and allow to cool (or add an ice cube to speed up the process).

4　Spoon some cooked alphabet pasta into each bowl of soup and sprinkle with a little grated Parmesan cheese if desired.

Technique Tip

Help your child use a sawing motion to move the child-safe knife back and forth to get through food with tougher skin, like bell peppers, limes, or tomatoes.

CRUNCHY FISH TACO BOWLS WITH SIMPLE GUACAMOLE

Level 3

Active time: 30 mins.
Cook time: 15 mins.

Dairy-free, egg-free, gluten-free

Serves 4

My four-year-old, Henry, loves helping me make guacamole, mostly because he loves sneaking spoonfuls of it when I'm not looking. This healthy and flavorful dinner contains a few components, but they all come together pretty quickly. For weeknight dinners, I like to get some help from the store and buy precooked frozen rice and quinoa. My boys still aren't huge quinoa fans but they love rice, so I usually make a mix of brown rice and quinoa.

1 pound firm white fish fillets, such as cod, haddock, or tilapia

2 cups corn tortilla chips

½ teaspoon garlic powder, divided

¼ teaspoon chili powder

2 teaspoons extra-virgin olive oil, divided

3 cups cooked quinoa, brown rice, or a mix of both

Zest and juice of one lime, divided

½ teaspoon plus pinch salt, divided, plus more if needed

1 pint grape tomatoes, halved lengthwise

2 cups frozen corn, thawed

2 ripe avocados, halved and pitted

¼ cup fresh cilantro leaves (optional)

1   Preheat the oven to 400°F. Line a baking sheet with parchment paper or aluminum foil and place the fish fillets on top.

We Made This Recipe On:

We Enjoyed:

We Rate This Recipe:
☆ ☆ ☆ ☆ ☆

Recipe Notes:

There's more ➡

2 Place the chips in a small zip-top plastic bag. Together, seal the bag tightly. Use a measuring cup or small rolling pin to crush the chips into a fine powder. Open the bag and add ¼ teaspoon garlic powder and the chili powder. Gently shake the bag to mix together.

3 Drizzle the fish with 1 teaspoon of olive oil and use the back of a spoon to spread it over the surface of the fish. Sprinkle the crushed chips over the fish to cover entirely. Pat the crust down gently to adhere. If there are lots of crumbs around the fish, gather them up and sprinkle them back on top. Wash hands.

4 Bake until the fish easily flakes apart, 10 to 15 minutes.

5 While the fish is cooking, put the cooked quinoa or rice in a large bowl. Together, use a Microplane or other small zester to zest the lime into the quinoa, then cut the lime in half and squeeze half of the lime over top. Add ¼ teaspoon of salt and mix to combine.

6 Using a child-safe knife, cut the tomatoes in half again and transfer them to a medium bowl with the corn. Add the remaining teaspoon of olive oil and a big pinch of salt and mix together. Into another bowl, scoop the avocado out of the skin with a spoon. Add about 1 tablespoon of lime juice and the remaining ¼ teaspoon of salt and ¼ teaspoon of garlic powder. Use a potato masher or the back of a fork to mash the guacamole. Together, taste and add more lime juice or salt as needed.

7 To serve, lay out all the taco bowl components and allow everyone to make their own bowl or plate. Sprinkle fresh cilantro leaves over top if desired.

ROASTED SHRIMP AND VEGGIE SUSHI RICE BOWLS

"Bowl" meals are a great way to make one dinner that pleases the whole family. Adults can pile everything in a bowl and drizzle it with sauce, and kiddos can enjoy the components separated, with the sauce on the side for dipping. Feel free to make this meal vegetarian by either leaving out the shrimp or using tofu instead. (Grown-up note: My husband and I also really like this meal with a drizzle of Sriracha hot sauce.)

2 cups uncooked sushi rice, rinsed

½ teaspoon salt

4 tablespoons rice vinegar, divided

2 large carrots

½ head cauliflower

3 teaspoons vegetable oil, divided

¼ teaspoon garlic powder

¼ cup low-sodium soy sauce or tamari

2 teaspoons honey

1 pound peeled and deveined large shrimp, defrosted if frozen, patted dry

½ English cucumber, halved lengthwise

1 avocado, halved, pitted, peeled, and quartered

2 sheets nori or 1 package toasted seaweed snacks

Level 2

Active time: 20 mins.
Cook time: 45 mins.

Dairy-free, egg-free,
gluten-free, nut-free

Serves 4

We made this recipe on:

We enjoyed:

We rate this recipe:

☆ ☆ ☆ ☆ ☆

Recipe notes:

There's more ➡

1. Preheat the oven to 425°F.

2. In a medium saucepan, combine the rice with 2¼ cups water and the salt. Bring the mixture to a full boil, then reduce the heat to low, cover, and simmer for 15 minutes. Remove from the heat and let rest, covered, for 15 minutes. Add 3 tablespoons of vinegar to the rice and stir.

3. Peel the carrots with your child, and help her cut the carrots across into ¼-inch slices, then into sticks or small "fry" shapes.

4. Break the cauliflower apart into small florets. Place the carrots and cauliflower in a large bowl with 2 teaspoons of oil, and sprinkle with the garlic powder. Toss together, then spread into a single layer on a baking sheet.

5. In a small bowl, whisk the soy sauce, the remaining tablespoon of vinegar, and the honey. Put the shrimp in a large bowl. Pour 2 teaspoons of the sauce mixture and the remaining teaspoon of oil over the shrimp. Toss to coat.

6. Roast the carrots and cauliflower until golden brown, about 25 minutes. Remove from the oven and push the vegetables off to the sides. Add the shrimp to the center of the baking sheet in a single layer and return the sheet to the oven until the shrimp are cooked through, about 4 minutes.

7. Dice the cucumber and slice the avocado. Use child-safe scissors to cut the nori into strips.

8. Together, divide the rice among four bowls. Serve with the roasted vegetables, shrimp, cucumber, avocado, and nori on top, or separated into piles for the little ones. Drizzle with the remaining sauce or serve on the side for dipping.

Make It Fun!
Have your kid use mini cookie cutters to cut sliced cucumbers and carrots (before roasting) into fun shapes to top these bowls. It's surprising how much more interested toddlers will be in trying a new dish when fun shapes are involved!

Snacks & Sides

Have you ever met a toddler who didn't like snacks? Hah—I didn't think so! Make an activity out of snack time and cook something together! Whipping up homemade snacks like Green Toad Toasts (page 88) or Green Bean "Fries" (page 101) is also a great way to get more fruits and veggies into the day and make snacks a more balanced mini meal.

Broccoli-Cheddar Cornbread
Muffins, page 97

Level 1

Active time: 10 mins.

Gluten-free, nut-free, vegan

Serves 4

We made this recipe on:

We enjoyed:

We rate this recipe:

☆ ☆ ☆ ☆ ☆

Recipe notes:

GREEN TOAD TOASTS

This fun snack was inspired by a mighty frog character in a popular children's book called *Little Blue Truck*. We think of avocado as a savory ingredient, but it tastes really great with sweet things like fruit, too. You can choose to use sliced vegetables to decorate your little frogs, or use a mixture of whatever fruits and vegetables you have on hand. Any way you top it, this is a delicious and nutritious snack.

1 ripe avocado, halved and pitted

2 teaspoons freshly squeezed lemon juice

Pinch salt

4 rice cakes or toasted bread slices

1 small English cucumber or banana, sliced

Blueberries, for topping

Sliced black olives, for topping

3 or 4 strawberries, sliced

1 Use a spoon to scoop the avocado out of the skin into a small bowl. Mash the avocado with a potato masher or the back of a fork. Stir in the lemon juice and salt.

2 Spread the mashed avocado onto the rice cakes or toast. Decorate with sliced veggies and fruit. Use larger slices of cucumber or banana as eyes, then place a blueberry or slice of olive on top for the pupil. Make a smile and a little nose with strawberries or blueberries. Enjoy!

Make It Fun!
What other stories can you create matching snacks for? Making a snack inspired by your child's favorite story or movie character will make even the most hesitant eater more excited to try something new.

Level 1

Active time: 10 mins.

Gluten-free, nut-free, vegetarian

Makes 2 cups

We made this recipe on:

We enjoyed:

We rate this recipe:

☆ ☆ ☆ ☆ ☆

Recipe notes:

HOMEMADE YOGURT-RANCH DIP

My boys are much more likely to eat veggies when I serve this dip alongside them. In fact, I make a batch once a week to keep in the fridge. It's so easy to make, you'll never buy ranch dressing from the store again. We like to add some mayo to the dip to give it a more traditional ranch taste, but feel free to use all yogurt instead.

1 lemon, halved

1½ cups full-fat or 2% plain Greek yogurt

½ cup mayonnaise (or more yogurt)

1 teaspoon dried dill

½ teaspoon onion powder

½ teaspoon garlic powder

½ teaspoon paprika

1 teaspoon honey (optional)

Pinch salt

1 Juice the lemon into a small bowl using a juicer or lemon squeezer.

2 Measure 2 tablespoons of the lemon juice into a larger bowl. Add all of the remaining ingredients. Use a whisk to slowly stir everything together. Serve this dip chilled with favorite crunchy veggies or anything else you like for dipping.

We made this recipe on:

We enjoyed:

We rate this recipe:

☆ ☆ ☆ ☆ ☆

Recipe notes:

CAULIFLOWER "POPCORN"

No, it's not really popcorn, but it is the most fun and delicious way to enjoy cauliflower! Giving vegetable dishes a creative name is a great way to get kids more excited about cooking them. The turmeric powder gives the cauliflower a popcorn-like yellow hue (plus it tastes great), but use it carefully, as it can stain hands and clothes.

½ head cauliflower, large stem removed

1 tablespoon extra-virgin olive oil

1 tablespoon grated Parmesan cheese (optional)

⅛ teaspoon garlic powder

⅛ teaspoon ground turmeric (optional)

Kosher salt

Freshly ground black pepper

1 Preheat the oven to 450°F. Line a baking sheet with parchment paper or spray with cooking spray.

2 Break the cauliflower into small florets (the size of a piece of popcorn) and put in a large bowl. Discard any large stems. Drizzle the olive oil over the cauliflower and stir to coat. Sprinkle the cauliflower with the cheese (if using), garlic powder, and turmeric (if using). Add a big pinch of salt and a few grinds of black pepper. Stir to combine. Dump the cauliflower out onto the prepared sheet and spread into an even layer without any overlapping.

3 Roast, flipping once halfway through, until the cauliflower is well browned and a little crispy, about 20 minutes. Serve warm.

Technique Tip

Roasting is a wonderful gateway method to get kids (or reluctant adults) to love veggies. This cooking method is especially recommended for carrots, Brussels sprouts, green beans, broccoli, and butternut squash, but the sky's the limit!

CHUNKY MONKEY BARS

(Banana-Oat Bars with Walnuts and Chocolate Chips)

If you have a toddler at home, you probably have some overripe bananas lying around from time to time. This easy snack bar recipe is nutritious enough to eat any time of day and delicious enough to present as a low-sugar dessert. Mashing bananas is a super toddler-friendly kitchen technique and makes this recipe an especially fun one to make with any child. Feel free to substitute another nut, or make this recipe nut-free by replacing the almond butter with sunflower seed butter and the walnuts with pumpkin seeds.

3 very ripe bananas

3 tablespoons almond butter

1 teaspoon vanilla extract

1¾ cups quick oats (gluten-free if desired)

1 cup walnut pieces, finely chopped

2 tablespoons chia seeds (optional)

½ teaspoon ground cinnamon

Pinch fine sea salt

2 tablespoons mini chocolate chips (vegan if desired)

1 Preheat the oven to 350°F. Line a 9-inch square baking pan with parchment paper or spray with nonstick cooking spray.

Level 1

Active time: 20 mins.
Cook time: 25 mins.

Gluten-free, vegan

Makes 12 bars

We made this recipe on:

We enjoyed:

We rate this recipe:

☆ ☆ ☆ ☆ ☆

Recipe notes:

There's more

2 Peel the bananas and put them in a large bowl. Mash the bananas with a potato masher or the back of a fork until only a few small chunks remain. Stir in the almond butter and vanilla.

3 Add the oats, walnuts, chia seeds (if using), cinnamon, and salt to the bowl. Stir until well combined. The batter will be thick. Dump the batter into the prepared pan, spreading evenly with the back of a spoon or spatula. Sprinkle the chocolate chips over the batter and gently press them into the top.

4 Bake the bars until golden brown around the edges, 20 to 25 minutes. Allow to cool completely, then cut into 12 bars.

DID SOMEONE SAY BANANA?

Make It Fun!

Want to make this recipe extra exciting? Put the peeled bananas in a large plastic zip-top bag, seal it very well, then have your toddler mash the banana up with her hands. This is a great sensory activity that doesn't make any mess at all!

BROCCOLI-CHEDDAR CORNBREAD MUFFINS

Have you ever made savory muffins? They are a fun and delicious way to get veggies into your day! Serve them as a snack or even alongside your family's favorite soup or chili.

1 small to medium head broccoli, cut into florets

1 cup milk (any kind)

1 tablespoon apple cider vinegar

1 cup cornmeal

1 cup all-purpose or white whole-wheat flour

1½ teaspoons baking powder

½ teaspoon baking soda

½ teaspoon fine salt

4 tablespoons (½ stick) butter, melted

2 large eggs

2 tablespoons honey

¼ cup finely shredded whole or part-skim Cheddar cheese, plus more for sprinkling (optional)

1. Preheat the oven to 375°F.

2. Fill a standard muffin tin with paper cupcake liners.

3. Using a child-safe knife, finely chop enough broccoli florets to measure about ¾ cup. Set aside. Pour the milk into a liquid measuring cup and add the vinegar. Set aside for 5 minutes.

There's more ➡️

Level 2

Active time: 20 mins.
Cook time: 15 mins.

Nut-free, vegetarian

Makes 12 muffins

We made this recipe on:

We enjoyed:

We rate this recipe:

☆ ☆ ☆ ☆ ☆

Recipe notes:

4 Measure the cornmeal, flour, baking powder, baking soda, and salt into a large bowl, and gently whisk them together.

5 In another bowl, mix the butter, eggs, and honey. Add the milk and vinegar mixture and whisk to combine. Pour the liquid ingredients into the dry ingredients and mix together. Stir in the chopped broccoli and shredded cheese.

6 Together, scoop the batter into the prepared muffin tin, filling each hole about three-quarters full. Top each muffin with an additional sprinkle of cheese if desired.

7 Bake until golden brown on the top and cooked through, so that a toothpick inserted in the center of a cupcake comes out clean, about 15 minutes.

Heads Up

Broccoli can be tricky for small hands to chop, so have your child help break apart the florets, then practice sawing back and forth to trim the broccoli "leaves" off the "tree." Chop the broccoli alongside your little chef, and if he gets tired of cutting, he can always keep busy transferring the chopped broccoli to a measuring cup.

GREEN BEAN "FRIES"

My boys aren't huge green bean fans, but they gobble up these "fries" every time we make them. The beans go through an assembly line–style breading station, so they are crispy, crunchy, and completely addictive. Keep a couple of towels nearby as you prep, because those little fingers will get messy!

12 ounces green beans

1 cup whole-wheat or regular panko bread crumbs

2 tablespoons grated Parmesan cheese

½ teaspoon garlic powder

½ teaspoon paprika

¼ teaspoon kosher salt

1 teaspoon extra-virgin olive oil

2 large eggs

½ cup all-purpose flour

Ketchup or your favorite dipping sauce, for serving (optional)

1 Preheat the oven to 375°F. Line a baking sheet with parchment paper or coat with nonstick cooking spray.

2 Trim the ends off the green beans with child-safe scissors or knife. If the beans are very long, cut them in half.

3 In a large bowl, combine the bread crumbs, cheese, garlic powder, paprika, salt, and oil. Crack the eggs into a small bowl and mix with a fork. Put the flour in another small bowl.

There's more

Active time: 20 mins.
Cook time: 12 mins.

Nut-free, vegetarian

Serves 2 to 3

We made this recipe on:

We enjoyed:

We rate this recipe:

☆ ☆ ☆ ☆ ☆

Recipe notes:

4 Together, make an assembly line with the three bowls: First, dip a green bean into the flour and shake off any excess. Next, dip the green bean into the egg, letting the excess drip off before placing it into the bread crumb mixture, turning the green bean around to coat evenly. Place the coated green bean on the baking sheet. Repeat with the remaining green beans. Arrange them on the baking sheet so they're not touching.

5 Bake for 12 minutes, or until the bread crumbs are golden brown. Serve warm or at room temperature with ketchup or another favorite dipping sauce if desired.

Make It Fun!

Love the crunchy coating on these green beans? Try the same recipe with other veggies, like zucchini sticks, cauliflower florets, or eggplant slices. Yum!

HONEY-WHEAT
SOFT PRETZEL STICKS

Does your toddler love playing with dough? This recipe comes together so easily, you'll want to make your own fresh pretzel sticks every week. Play with the toppings and switch out the salt on top for a sprinkle of cinnamon and sugar, or make them more savory and put some "everything" bagel seasoning on top to make bagel sticks. The delicious snack you create together will be well worth getting your hands a little messy.

1 cup white whole-wheat flour or ½ cup all-purpose flour and ½ cup whole-wheat flour

2 teaspoons baking powder

½ teaspoon fine salt

1 cup plain Greek yogurt

1 tablespoon honey

1 large egg

Kosher salt

1. Preheat the oven to 375°F. Line a baking sheet with parchment paper or coat with nonstick cooking spray.

2. In a large bowl, combine the flour, baking powder, and salt and whisk together. Add the yogurt and honey. Use a fork or spatula to mix until a rough dough forms.

There's more

Level 3

Active time: 20 mins.
Cook time: 20 mins.

Nut-free, vegetarian

Makes 4 pretzel sticks

We made this recipe on:

We enjoyed:

We rate this recipe:

☆ ☆ ☆ ☆ ☆

Recipe notes:

3 Dust a work surface with a little flour, dump the dough out onto the flour, and use hands to bring the dough together into a ball. Knead for a minute or so until the dough is smooth, taking turns if desired.

4 Together, form the dough into a log and cut into 4 equal pieces. Roll each piece into a 6-inch stick and place on the prepared baking sheet.

5 Crack the egg into a small bowl and beat with a fork. Use a pastry brush to brush each pretzel stick with the egg. Sprinkle a big pinch of salt over each stick.

6 Bake the pretzel sticks until golden brown, about 20 minutes. Serve warm or at room temperature.

Technique Tip

Teach kids to knead dough with the heel of their hands and not squish the dough between their fingers. Using a closed hand will make the process a little less messy.

RAINBOW BLACK BEAN SALSA WITH BAKED CHIPS

Level 3

Active time: 30 mins.
Cook time: 12 mins.

Gluten-free, nut-free, vegan

Serves 4

Here's another delicious way to "eat the rainbow"! Raw zucchini might seem like a strange ingredient to add to salsa, but we like its mild taste, and it's super easy to cut with a child-safe knife. Since there's a lot of chopping, this recipe is best for toddlers with a little more kitchen experience. However, making the chips is a great activity to do with any child.

2 large plum tomatoes or 1 cup grape tomatoes

½ orange bell pepper, seeds and ribs removed

½ yellow bell pepper, seeds and ribs removed

½ zucchini, ends trimmed

2 tablespoons extra-virgin olive oil, divided

6 corn tortillas

1 (15-ounce) can black beans, drained and rinsed

1 lime, halved

¼ cup fresh cilantro leaves

¼ teaspoon garlic powder

¼ teaspoon kosher salt, plus more for seasoning

1   Preheat the oven to 375°F. Line a baking sheet with parchment paper or aluminum foil.

2   Prepare the vegetables so they are easier for a child to cut: Cut the tomatoes into wedges or halves, slice the peppers into thin strips, and cut the zucchini into thin sticks.

We made this recipe on:

We enjoyed:

We rate this recipe:

☆ ☆ ☆ ☆ ☆

Recipe notes:

There's more

3 Pour 1 tablespoon of oil into a small bowl. Use a pastry brush to paint both sides of all the tortillas with a thin layer of oil.

4 Together, using a pizza wheel or knife, cut each tortilla into 8 wedges. Place the tortilla wedges onto the baking sheet without overlapping. Bake until golden brown, 10 to 12 minutes.

5 Using a child-safe knife, chop the tomatoes, peppers, and zucchini into a small dice and put in a large bowl. Add the beans, then squeeze the juice of half the lime over the top. Rip up the cilantro with your fingers or snip with child-safe scissors and add to the bowl. Add the remaining 1 tablespoon of oil, the garlic powder, and salt. Stir to combine. Together, taste the salsa and add more lime juice or salt as needed. Serve with the chips.

Desserts

There's no doubt about it: Kids love making desserts! Can you blame them? Everyone needs a sweet treat once in a while, and all of these recipes, from Mini PB&J Cupcakes (page 127) to Chocolate Pudding "Dirt" Cups (page 123), are great to make and share. Bring them to a party or play date to enjoy with friends!

6

Level 1

Active time: 20 mins.

Egg-free, gluten-free, nut-free, vegetarian

Makes 8 pops

We made this recipe on:

We enjoyed:

We rate this recipe:

☆ ☆ ☆ ☆ ☆

Recipe notes:

FROZEN WATERMELON "PIZZA" POPS

A refreshing summer treat, these pops couldn't be easier to make. Just freeze the watermelon the day before, put out some toppings, and you are ready to party! Feel free to make the recipe without the ice pop sticks. Fingers might get a little cold, but the treats will be just as delicious.

1 large wedge watermelon (about 2 pounds)

½ cup plain Greek yogurt

2 teaspoons honey

Thinly sliced strawberries, blueberries, sprinkles, and/or mini chocolate chips, for topping

1 Cut the watermelon into 8 pizza-like wedges. Use the tip of a sharp knife to make a small slice in the center of the watermelon rind. Make the slit just big enough for a wooden ice pop stick to fit inside. Place the ice pop sticks three-quarters of the way through each wedge of watermelon. Place the watermelon pops on a baking sheet lined with parchment paper or wax paper. Place in the freezer for at least 2 hours or overnight.

2 Put the yogurt in a small bowl, and stir in the honey. Remove the watermelon from the freezer and spread a spoonful of yogurt on top of each slice, like pizza "sauce."

3 Decorate the watermelon slices with the toppings of your choice. Enjoy immediately or place back in the freezer to enjoy later.

PUMPKIN CHOCOLATE CHIP COOKIES

Level 1

Active time: 15 mins.
Cook time: 12 mins.

Nut-free, vegan

Makes 14 small cookies

Making chocolate chip cookies is basically a childhood rite of passage, right? This recipe is the perfect one to make with a first-time baker. There are no eggs, so you don't have to worry about your little one sampling the dough, and the pumpkin purée adds a little extra boost of nutrients. Substitute oat flour or all-purpose gluten-free flour to make them gluten-free.

½ cup canned pumpkin (not pumpkin pie filling)

¼ cup vegetable oil

¼ cup brown sugar or coconut sugar

1 teaspoon pumpkin pie spice or ground cinnamon

¼ teaspoon fine salt

¾ cup whole-wheat or all-purpose flour

½ teaspoon baking powder

½ teaspoon baking soda

¼ cup mini chocolate chips (vegan if desired)

1   Preheat the oven to 350°F. Line a baking sheet with parchment paper or spray with nonstick cooking spray.

2 Put the pumpkin, oil, sugar, pumpkin pie spice, and salt in a large bowl. Whisk to combine.

We made this recipe on:

We enjoyed:

We rate this recipe:

☆☆☆☆☆

Recipe notes:

There's more ➜

3 Add the flour, baking powder, and baking soda to the bowl. Use a wooden spoon or spatula to stir all the ingredients together. Stir in the chocolate chips.

4 Scoop tablespoon-size balls of dough onto the prepared baking sheet. Flatten gently with the back of a spoon or your hands.

5 Bake until puffed and lightly golden around the edges, about 12 minutes. Cool completely before serving.

Technique Tip

Teach your little baker to whisk and stir properly: One hand holds the bowl still, while the other holds the stirring utensil. Stir by moving your wrist, not your whole arm, so the ingredients stay in the bowl.

TRAIL MIX KRISPY TREATS

Level 2

Active time: 20 mins.

Egg-free, vegetarian

Makes 16 squares

Another kid favorite with a fun and delicious spin!
Play with the mix-ins and include whatever your
family likes in their trail mix. Nuts, seeds, dried fruit,
chocolate chips—what will you put in yours? These
are the perfect treats to bring to a school gathering or
family get-together. You can easily make them nut-free
by omitting the almonds, and gluten-free by using
gluten-free pretzels.

4 tablespoons (½ stick) unsalted butter

¼ cup packed light brown sugar

¼ cup honey

½ teaspoon kosher salt

2 cups pretzel sticks

3 cups crispy rice cereal

1 cup roasted sunflower kernels (salted
or unsalted)

½ cup sliced almonds

½ cup dried cranberries or raisins

1   Line an 8-inch square baking pan with parchment paper or aluminum foil.

2 Put the butter, brown sugar, honey, and salt in
a small pot.

3   Place the pot on the stove over medium-high
heat. Once the butter is melted and the mixture
starts to boil, turn off the heat and set the pot aside.
Do not boil the mixture for more than 1 minute or it
will be too hard to pour onto the cereal.

There's more ➡

We made this recipe on:

We enjoyed:

We rate this recipe:
☆ ☆ ☆ ☆ ☆

Recipe notes:

4 Put the pretzel sticks in a small zip-top plastic bag and seal tightly. Use the bottom of a measuring cup or a small rolling pin to crush the pretzels into small pieces. Put the crushed pretzels, the rice cereal, sunflower kernels, almonds, and cranberries in a large bowl, and mix gently with a large spoon or spatula.

5 Pour the butter mixture over the rice cereal mixture in the bowl. Stir briefly to combine, then allow your child to help mix everything together. Make sure all the cereal and mix-ins are coated with the butter mixture.

6 Together, pour the mixture into the prepared pan and spread evenly. Place an additional piece of parchment paper or foil on top of the mixture in the pan and use your hands to flatten the top and make it as even as possible.

7 Place the pan in the freezer for 15 minutes or refrigerate for about an hour to cool completely. Once cool, cut into 16 squares.

Heads Up

The butter mixture will be very hot after it's cooked. The safest option is to keep it away from kids while you pour it over the cereal mixture. After you pour it and give the cereal a stir, little ones can then safely help.

NO-BAKE
COOKIE DOUGH BITES

Cookie dough that's safe to eat and easy to make? Yes! Substitute any nut or seed butter for the almond butter, and add in colored sprinkles, raisins, dried cranberries, or whatever you'd like to customize these little treats.

1 cup old-fashioned rolled oats (gluten-free if desired)

½ cup unsweetened almond butter

3 tablespoons maple syrup

½ teaspoon vanilla extract

¼ teaspoon fine salt

1 tablespoon water

¼ cup mini chocolate chips (vegan if desired)

1 Together, put the oats in a food processor and grind into a fine powder. (We like to sing our ABCs while this happens.)

2 Add the almond butter, maple syrup, vanilla, salt, and water to the food processor. Together, process until a dough forms.

3 Check the dough to make sure it rolls into a ball nicely. If it's too dry, add some additional water and process again. If too sticky, add another tablespoon of oats and process again.

We made this recipe on:

We enjoyed:

We rate this recipe:
☆ ☆ ☆ ☆ ☆

Recipe notes:

There's more

4 Add the mini chocolate chips and, together, pulse a few times to mix.

5 Remove the blade from the food processor and set it away from your work area.

6 Roll the dough into teaspoon-size balls and place in an airtight container for storage, either at room temperature or, for firmer cookies, in the refrigerator.

Heads Up

Little hands may have trouble rolling dough into round balls. Let them experiment with whatever shape cookie dough bites they'd like to make. If the cookie dough is sticking to your hands, rub a little oil on them to make rolling the balls a bit easier.

I'M WILD FOR COOKIE DOUGH!

CHOCOLATE PUDDING "DIRT" CUPS

This dessert is so fun and yummy, the kiddos won't even know it's way healthier than the original chocolate pudding and crushed cookie version. Make these pudding cups for a family get-together or play date. Even avocado skeptics will be pleasantly surprised by this sweet treat!

½ cup rolled oats (gluten-free if desired)

2 tablespoons unsweetened coconut flakes

¼ cup unsweetened cocoa powder, divided

¼ cup honey or maple syrup, plus 1 tablespoon

2 teaspoons vegetable or coconut oil

2 ripe avocados, halved and pitted

3 tablespoons coconut milk (or any kind of milk)

Pinch salt

½ teaspoon vanilla extract

Fresh mint and/or dye-free gummy worms, for topping (optional)

1 Make the "dirt": Put the oats, coconut, 1 tablespoon of cocoa powder, 1 tablespoon of honey, and the oil in a food processor. Together, pulse until a crumbly, dirt-looking mixture forms.

2 Remove the blade from the food processor and scrape the dirt mixture into a bowl. Set aside. Return the blade and food processor bowl to the base.

There's more ➡

Level 2

Active time: 30 mins.

Gluten-free, nut-free, vegan

Serves 4

We made this recipe on:

We enjoyed:

We rate this recipe:

☆ ☆ ☆ ☆ ☆

Recipe notes:

3 For the pudding, spoon the avocado flesh out of the skin into a small bowl. Add the avocado to the food processor, along with the milk, the remaining 3 tablespoons of cocoa powder and ¼ cup of honey, the salt, and vanilla. Together, blend until smooth. Refrigerate until ready to assemble the cups.

4 Scoop the pudding into small glasses or cups and smooth the top with the back of a spoon to make level. Crumble some chocolate dirt on top. You may not need to use all the dirt. Stick a sprig of mint in the top as the plant in the dirt and place some gummy worms on top, if you wish. Serve chilled.

Make It Fun!

Sensory play! Take any extra "dirt"—even make a few additional batches—put it in a big bin or baking pan, add some little trucks, and you've got a fun (and sweet!) activity to keep little ones busy. Sensory play also exposes children to different textures and sensations, which can often prevent or help with picky eating.

MINI PB&J CUPCAKES

With its beloved kid flavors, this one-bowl peanut butter cake and easy strawberry jelly frosting combine to make a party-worthy treat. Make these cupcakes extra fancy and play around with the toppings: Add some chopped peanuts for crunch or a slice of fresh strawberry to the top to make the mini cakes look picture-perfect!

8 tablespoons (1 stick) butter, divided
1 large egg
⅓ cup packed light brown sugar
3 tablespoons creamy peanut butter
1 teaspoon vanilla extract
¼ cup milk
¾ cup all-purpose flour
½ teaspoon baking powder
½ cup cream cheese, at room temperature
¾ cup confectioners' sugar
¼ cup strawberry jam, divided
Sliced strawberries, for topping (optional)
Chopped peanuts, for topping (optional)

1   Melt 4 tablespoons of butter and set aside to cool. Preheat the oven to 350°F.

2   Cut the remaining 4 tablespoons of butter into 8 pieces and leave on the counter to soften. Line 18 holes of a mini-cupcake pan with paper liners.

Level 3

Active time: 30 mins.
Cook time: 8 mins.

Vegetarian
Makes 16 to 18 mini cupcakes

We made this recipe on:

We enjoyed:

We rate this recipe:
☆ ☆ ☆ ☆ ☆

Recipe notes:

There's more ➡

3 Crack the egg into a large bowl. Add the melted butter, brown sugar, peanut butter, vanilla, and milk. Whisk until smooth and well combined.

4 Add the flour and baking powder to the bowl. Stir with a wooden spoon or spatula until just combined and no streaks of flour remain. Work together to spoon the batter into the prepared pan, filling each cupcake liner about three-quarters of the way.

5 Bake until the cupcakes are cooked through and a toothpick inserted in the center of a cupcake comes out clean, about 8 minutes. Allow to cool in the pan for 5 minutes, then transfer the cupcakes to a cooling rack to cool completely.

6 To make the frosting, put the softened butter, cream cheese, confectioners' sugar, and 3 tablespoons of strawberry jam in a large bowl. With an adult's help, use a handheld mixer to beat the ingredients until light and fluffy. Scoop the frosting into a small zip-top plastic bag and seal the top. Together, snip a corner off the bag and pipe some frosting around the edge of each cupcake, leaving a small spot in the center empty. Spoon a tiny bit more of the remaining 1 tablespoon strawberry jam into the open spot in the center of each cupcake. Top with the strawberries and peanuts, if desired.

7 If the frosting is getting too soft, place in the refrigerator for a few minutes. Store the decorated cupcakes in the refrigerator until ready to eat.

measurement conversions

Oven Temperatures

Fahrenheit (F)	Celsius (C) (approx.)
250°F	120°C
300°F	150°C
325°F	165°C
350°F	180°C
375°F	190°C
400°F	200°C
425°F	220°C
450°F	230°C

Volume Equivalents (Liquid)

Standard	US Standard (oz.)	Metric (approx.)
2 tablespoons	1 fl. oz.	30 mL
¼ cup	2 fl. oz.	60 mL
½ cup	4 fl. oz.	120 mL
1 cup	8 fl. oz.	240 mL
1½ cups	12 fl. oz.	355 mL
2 cups or 1 pint	16 fl. oz.	475 mL
4 cups or 1 quart	32 fl. oz.	1 L
1 gallon	128 fl. oz.	4 L

Weight Equivalents

Standard	Metric (approx.)
½ ounce	15 g
1 ounce	30 g
2 ounces	60 g
4 ounces	115 g
8 ounces	225 g
12 ounces	340 g
16 ounces or 1 pound	455 g

Volume Equivalents (Dry)

Standard	Metric (approx.)
⅛ teaspoon	0.5 mL
¼ teaspoon	1 mL
½ teaspoon	2 mL
¾ teaspoon	4 mL
1 teaspoon	5 mL
1 tablespoon	15 mL
¼ cup	59 mL
⅓ cup	79 mL
½ cup	118 mL
⅔ cup	156 mL
¾ cup	177 mL
1 cup	235 mL
2 cups or 1 pint	475 mL
3 cups	700 mL
4 cups or 1 quart	1 L

recipe level index

index

acknowledgments

To my husby, Kyle, thank you for always giving me honest feedback and encouraging me to be a better version of myself everyday while still loving me just the way I am. Thank you for taking care of our monkeys when I was buried in my laptop. You are the best dad.

Thank you to my parents, who taught me what unconditional love really looks and feels like. You gave me a childhood filled with wonderful food and culinary experiences, and I would not have my passion for cooking and teaching without you. Jack and Henry are so lucky to have you in their lives.

To my siblings, Stacey, Jon, Lindsey, and Nathanial, I love you.

Breana, Jacob, Donna, and Norman, I don't know what I would do without you. Thank you for always taking the best care of the boys. You are the best family I could ever hope for.

Thank you Jo, Renee, and the Create a Cook family. There's no way I would be writing a book about cooking with kids if it weren't for all those years of guidance, friendship, and moping.

Thank you to my Bowdoin girls for your help, love, and true friendship.

Thank you to some of my most loyal cheerleaders and friends, Marissa, Katie, Sarah, Robin, and Nicole D.

Thank you to my Instagram squad for endless support in business and motherhood. A special thanks to those of you who tried and tested my recipes, especially Kelly, Jennifer, Megan, and Lisa. Thank you, Taesha and Krista, for always listening and being such supportive friends.

Big thanks to the Callisto team for giving me this opportunity I've always dreamed of—helping parents and toddlers everywhere cook and learn together.

about the author

Heather Wish Staller is a cooking instructor, recipe developer, Instagram lover, and mom of two boys. She has a passion for getting kids into the kitchen and helping parents raise happy, healthy eaters and future home chefs. After attending Bowdoin College (where she met her husband) and taking lots of art and education classes, she decided to fulfill her lifelong dream of attending culinary school. Heather enjoyed working at restaurants and as a private chef after school, but found true happiness teaching cooking to kids at a recreational cooking school. After working at that school for 10 years, Heather started her own business teaching cooking in preschools and educational centers in her area. She also works at home part-time developing recipes for brand partnerships and other collaborations. When Heather's not cooking with her favorite ingredients—cream cheese, avocado, and kale—she is spending time with her boys and husband at their home by the beach outside Boston. Visit Heather's website, HappyKidsKitchen.com, and @heather.happykidskitchen on Instagram to join a wonderful community of food-loving parents.

Printed in the USA
CPSIA information can be obtained
at www.ICGtesting.com
LVHW060528040124
767690LV00002B/47

9 781641 524766